The Pueblo

CHRISTA BEDRY

PRINCIPAL PHOTOGRAPHY BY MARILYN "ANGEL" WYNN

CHELSEA
CLUBHOUSE
An Imprint of Chelsea House Publishers
A Haights Cross Communications Company
Philadelphia

This edition first published in 2004 in the United States of America by Chelsea Clubhouse, a division of Chelsea House Publishers and a subsidiary of Haights Cross Communications.

Chelsea Clubhouse
1974 Sproul Road, Suite 400
Broomall, PA 19008-0914

The Chelsea House world wide web address is www.chelseahouse.com

Library of Congress Cataloging-in-Publication Data

Bedry, Christa.
   The Pueblo / Christa Bedry.
      v. cm. -- (American Indian art and culture)
Includes bibliographical references and index.
Contents: The people -- Pueblo homes -- Pueblo communities -- Pueblo clothing -- Pueblo food -- Tools and technology -- Pueblo religion -- Ceremonies and celebrations -- Music and dance -- Language and storytelling -- Pueblo art -- Special feature -- Studying the Pueblos' past.
   ISBN 0-7910-7964-3 (Chelsea House) (lib. bdg. : alk. paper)
1. Pueblo Indians--History--Juvenile literature. 2. Pueblo Indians--Social life and customs--Juvenile literature. [1. Pueblo Indians.] I. Title. II. Series.
   E99.P9B379 2004
   978.9004'9749--dc22

                                       2003017518
                    Printed in the United States of America
                    1 2 3 4 5 6 7 8 9 0 07 06 05 04 03

©2004 WEIGL EDUCATIONAL PUBLISHERS LIMITED

Project Coordinator Heather C. Hudak **Substantive Editor** Jennifer Nault **Design** Janine Vangool
Layout Terry Paulhus **Photo Researcher** Wendy Cosh **Chelsea Clubhouse Editors** Sally Cheney
and Margaret Brierton **Validator** Lena Tsethlikia

Please note
At the time of printing, the Internet addresses appearing in this book were correct. Owing to the dynamic nature of the Internet, however, we cannot guarantee that all these addresses will remain correct.

CONTENTS

The People

More than 1,000 years ago, a group of American Indians called the Pueblo peoples lived in small villages made of stone and mud in northwestern New Mexico and northeastern Arizona. They belonged to four separate language groups called **dialects**, but their way of life was quite similar. This is because they shared the same history. Their **ancestors**, the Ancestral **Puebloans** (Anasazi) settled and farmed in the Four Corners region of the Southwest between about A.D. 1 and A.D. 1300.

In 1540, Spanish explorer Francisco Vasquez de Coronado traveled through the American southwest. He called the people who lived in permanent towns "Pueblos" after their unusual dwellings. Pueblo means "town" in the Spanish language.

Long ago, the Pueblo peoples' livelihood depended on farming and trading in western and central New Mexico, eastern Arizona, and

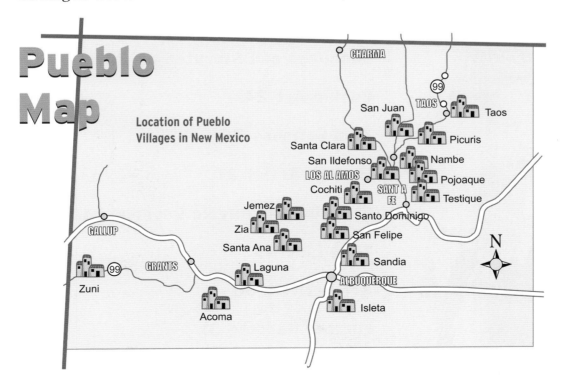

Pueblo Map

Location of Pueblo Villages in New Mexico

western Texas. They built pueblo villages along the rocky edges of canyons. This allowed them to save the nearby farmland for their crops. It also enabled them to stay close to the rivers running through the canyon below.

Today, most Pueblo peoples live in cities. Others live in the few remaining pueblos along the Rio Grande River in New Mexico. The Western Pueblos include Hopi and Zuni peoples. Hopi peoples live on three **mesas** in northeast Arizona. The Zuni peoples live in a very large pueblo in western New Mexico. Traditionally, Puebloans who have left their villages make return visits in order to carry on their cultural traditions.

In pueblo villages, people gather in the plazas to dance and celebrate.

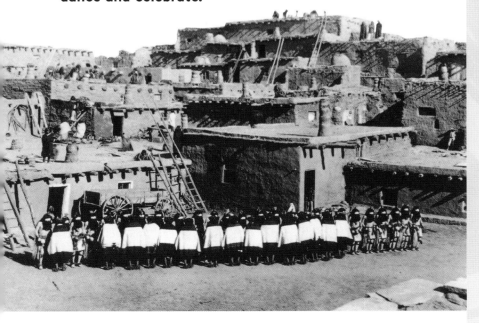

Modern-day Puebloans make a living in a variety of ways. Many find jobs outside the villages. Many of those who stay in the village have farms and raise crops of corn, beans, squash, chilies, tomatoes, and other vegetables. Others make pottery, jewelry, blankets, or baskets just as their ancestors did. In each village, these tools and pieces of art have their own style and design.

Artists display their pottery at American Indian markets.

Pueblo Homes

Imagine living in a house that is 100 years old. Today, some Pueblo peoples live in much older homes. Their pueblo dwellings look much like the homes their ancestors built hundreds of years ago.

Pueblo houses look like apartments, which are stacked on top of one another like a staircase. Each family's house consists of a few connected rooms. In the past, people entered pueblo houses through a trapdoor in the roof. They used ladders to get to the roof. Today, pueblo houses have hinged doors and glass windows, which face toward a central **plaza**. Some very large pueblos have more than one plaza.

The walls of pueblo homes are made from stones or blocks that are covered with **adobe** mud. The solid mud walls and roofs of pueblo houses are thick. This keeps the houses cool inside, even when the weather is hot. The inner walls of pueblo houses are covered with a layer of white mud called **gypsum**. This keeps the home clean and bright.

Traditionally, pueblo homes had thick, flat roofs.

DWELLING AND DECORATION

Pueblo peoples placed large logs called *vigas* across the top of their houses to support the flat roofs. Flat roofs provided an extra space where people could visit or work. They took vigas from nearby mountain forests and hauled them to the desert. The ends of the logs usually pointed beyond the top ledges of the house, through the adobe wall. Vigas were covered with small sticks, grass mats, and mud.

Many Pueblo peoples still live on community land. However, some villagers live in modern houses outside the original pueblo villages. Many return to their villages for ceremonies and other celebrations.

Pueblo Indians used ladders to climb from one level of the pueblo to another.

Pueblo Communities

In many ways, the Pueblo peoples' lifestyle has not changed much over the years. They still follow many of their cultural traditions. However, modern life has had an effect on the Pueblo peoples. Changes in transportation, work methods, tools, and other recent conveniences have made their way into Pueblo life. Although many villagers now work beyond Pueblo land, most still practice the traditions of their ancestors, including ceremonies and art.

For generations, Pueblo Indians have cultivated beans, corn, squash, and other vegetables in family waffle gardens. This type of garden is ideally suited for agriculture in the dry southwestern United States.

Because living in a dry region can be difficult, the Pueblo peoples had to cooperate to survive. They worked together and performed jobs according to a schedule. If one family's crops failed, they relied on neighbors and other family members for help.

Pueblo men cleared the fields and prepared the soil for planting. Men wove cloth and baskets, built houses, and led ceremonies. Pueblo women did most of the farming. They used sharp sticks to poke holes in the soil. Then they dropped seeds into the holes and covered them over with dirt. Women also prepared food, cared for the children, made pottery, and transported water. They also helped the men build houses and weave baskets and clothing. Pueblo children worked in the fields.

Each village had its own government and land area. In early history, the town government had a **council**, which was ruled by an elected chief. Pueblo priests were community leaders. They were responsible for handing out medicine to villagers. They also decided when the village would go to war or hunt.

Today, a tribal governor and war chief are chosen each year by the Tribal Council. This council consists of a group of 50 elders. The governor and his staff address local issues within the village and oversee relations with non-American Indians. The war chief and his staff work to protect the mountains and American-Indian lands beyond the pueblo village walls.

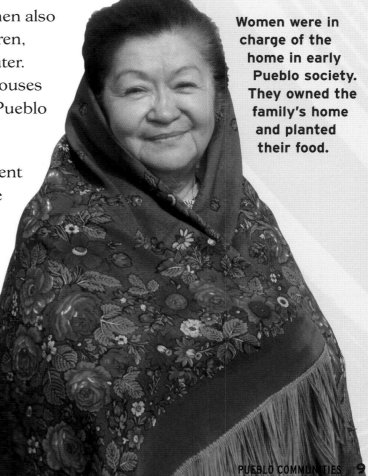

Women were in charge of the home in early Pueblo society. They owned the family's home and planted their food.

Pueblo Clothing

Long ago, most Pueblo peoples made their clothes from woven cloth, rather than the animal hides other American Indian nations used. Some tribes in colder areas used animal hides for clothing. Their ancestors, the Ancestral Puebloans, had been growing, spinning, dying, and weaving cotton since at least A.D. 800. When the Spanish settlers arrived and brought sheep, the Puebloans began spinning sheep's wool into yarn to make clothing.

Today, young Pueblo Indians take pride in dressing in traditional clothing.

Men and boys wore shirts, along with loose pants or short skirts. Women and girls wore blankets called **mantas**, which had one strap over the right shoulder. They wore colorful dresses or long sleeved shirts beneath the mantas.

In the warm summer months, Pueblo peoples did not wear many clothes. In fact, children younger than 10 years of age did not have to wear clothing. Men wore a breechcloth, which was a piece of leather or cloth tied around their waist. Women wore cotton or wool dresses. In the winter, the Pueblo peoples draped warm, woven blankets around themselves. The Puebloans also weaved colorful sashes. These long strips of cloth could be tied as belts to hold the blankets in place.

Puebloan men and women often decorate themselves with tattoos and jewelry. They make jewelry from **turquoise**, **obsidian**, shells, coral, and silver. Necklaces, bracelets, and earrings are common pieces of jewelry. Each pueblo has its own style of jewelry making. Experienced art collectors can tell which pueblo a piece of jewelry or art came from, just by looking at the style of the piece.

Long ago, Puebloans went barefoot. Beginning in A.D. 500 to 700, they wove sandals made from the **yucca** plant and moccasins of deerskin. The moccasins worn by the Pueblo peoples were unique. Most nations wore low moccasins around the foot. But the Puebloans wore high ones that went up the calf. Men wore their moccasins above the ankle. Women wore their moccasins slightly below the knee. They wrapped white deerskin around their legs up to their knees. The hard soles of all moccasins were bent slightly up and over the side of the foot.

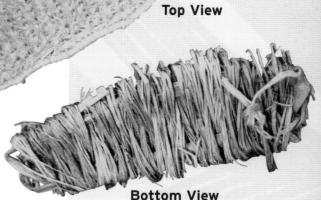

Top View

Bottom View

Yucca leaves were the primary source of material used in Pueblo sandals.

Pueblo Food

For hundreds of years, the Pueblo peoples have had a wide and varied diet. Ancestral Puebloans tamed turkeys and raised them for meat and eggs. Sometimes they hunted antelope, birds, deer, elks, prairie dogs, and rabbits. Ancestral Puebloans were also some of the first farmers in North America. Because they lived in dry desert areas, they had to create farming methods to maintain their crops of beans, corn, and squash. Most importantly, they found ways to **irrigate**, or bring water to, their fields. Later, Spanish settlers introduced the Pueblo peoples to fruits, chilies, onions, and tomatoes.

Corn was one of the Pueblo peoples' most important crops. Pueblo women ground up the corn and made it into flat breads called tortillas. They cooked tortillas and other foods in a *horno*. These dome-shaped ovens were built by covering bricks with mud. Pueblo peoples sometimes still use these traditional ovens today.

Corn came in many varieties and colors. Farmers often passed their own special corn varieties down to their sons. Blue corn, which grows on smaller cobs than yellow corn, is special to the Pueblo. Many of their recipes call for blue corn. Follow the recipe below to make blue corn tortillas. If you cannot find blue cornmeal, you can replace it with yellow cornmeal.

The Pueblo ate seeds, beans, squash, and corn. Nearly 80 percent of the Pueblo diet contained corn.

Blue Corn Tortillas

Ingredients:

1/3 cup (78.9 ml) flour

1 cup (236.6 ml) water

1–2/3 cup (394.3 ml) blue or yellow cornmeal

Equipment:

large bowl

wax paper

pan

spatula

rolling pin

1. Stir all the ingredients together in a large bowl.

2. Make 12 dough balls. Flatten the balls into tortillas by rolling each ball between two sheets of greased wax paper. You can also pat the ball between your hands until it is a thin tortilla.

3. Cook the tortilla in a lightly greased pan. Heat each side until it is a light brown color.

4. Remove from heat, let cool, and enjoy.

Tools, Weapons, and Defense

The Pueblo peoples used tools to make their tasks easier. Pueblo women used tools for grinding corn. A Pueblo woman cut dried corn kernels off the cob. She placed the corn kernels on a *matate*, a large, flat stone that had a dent in the center. A smaller stone called a *mano* was rolled over the matate to grind the corn. After the kernels were ground once, they were moved to smoother stones, and the process was repeated.

To farm in their fields, the Pueblo peoples used wooden digging sticks. They used hoes made from stone or animal bone to clear the land. Today, the Pueblo peoples use modern farming equipment.

The Pueblo peoples also created special tools for making pottery or weaving baskets and clothes. They used upright **looms** and wooden spindle whorls for weaving. A spindle is a wooden rod that is used to twist fibers into thread. The whorl is used to keep the spinning wheel moving at a regular speed. Other weaving tools included combs to press the threads down after they were woven into cloth, and spreader sticks to separate different threads as they were woven.

Scientists have found the remains of Pueblo tools, such as arrows and darts. Arrowheads were usually attached to shafts using animal tendon.

HUNTING AND HIDING

Before Spanish settlers arrived in North America, the Pueblo peoples used bows and arrows to hunt. Arrowheads and knives were made from rocks. Pueblo men flaked or shaped the rocks to make them sharp. Other weapons included the **lance**, club, and shield. Beautiful shields are still used during ceremonies.

The Pueblo peoples designed their villages to defend them against other American Indian nations. They made taller villages, and used the back walls of some houses to form one single wall around the village. A person could only gain entrance to these villages by climbing a ladder over the outer walls. When the ladders were brought inside, the pueblo village was protected from intruders.

The Zuni and Hopi defended themselves by building their villages on high mesas. It was hard for invaders to climb the steep sides of the mesas.

The Pueblo used the rabbit stick to hunt small game. The rabbit stick was designed to be a throwing club.

Pueblo Religion

The Pueblo respected nature and treated each other with kindness. They treated strangers well and tried to speak nicely to each other. They were truthful and respectful of their parents and seniors. Every part of Puebloan life was based on spirituality. As part of every activity, from planting, to building, to hunting, to chores, Pueblo peoples prayed and made offerings. They often used cornmeal as an offering to the spirits. People gathered in a round, underground room called a **kiva** for religious ceremonies.

When the Spanish settlers arrived, they punished the Puebloans who would not change their beliefs and become Christians. This forced Puebloans to practice their religion secretly. They believed that religion was a way to create **harmony** with the universe. But the Pueblo peoples knew becoming Christian would help establish harmony with the settlers. As a result, they were willing to add the new religion to their own religious beliefs. Some of the Christian saints were included in the **kachinas**. Today, many Pueblo peoples are Christians. However, they maintain some of their ancient beliefs.

The Christian mission San Francisco de Asis became a popular place for the nearby Pueblo to visit. Many of the Pueblo converted to Christianity at the mission.

KACHINAS

The Puebloans believed in spirits called kachinas. Throughout the year, they performed different ceremonies and dances for each spirit. Some of the ceremonies lasted for days. Adults gave kachina dolls to the children. These dolls were used to teach the children about their religion, how to do chores, or other lessons. There are more than 300 different types of kachina dolls.

The Pueblo still use kachina dolls as educational tools, but the dolls are also sold as art pieces.

Ceremonies and Celebrations

The Puebloans held important ceremonies throughout the year. Some ceremonies were based on Pueblo religion. Other ceremonies combined ancient southwestern traditions with the Catholic celebrations, which the Spanish settlers introduced. During ceremonies, the Puebloans performed complex dances. Each dance used specific movements to tell a story about an act of nature. For example, the Pueblo peoples performed a ceremony at each stage of the farming season. There were dances and ceremonies before planting. Once the crops were planted, there were other dances and ceremonies to bring rain and protect the crops. The biggest celebration came with the harvest of the crops. The Pueblo peoples perform the Corn Dance after the harvest. This was a dance of thanksgiving for the crop and a prayer for rain during the next farming season. The Puebloans also held ceremonies following a successful hunt, or to celebrate wisdom and strength.

Today, the main ceremonies are held in the kivas between crop seasons. They are ceremonies of prayer and thanksgiving for rain and good crops. Helpful spirits, called kachinas, are responsible for bringing rain and comfort to the people.

The Pueblo peoples believe these spirits **possess** the masked kachina dancers who perform in the ceremonies. Kachina dolls are carved from wood and clothed in masks and costumes so they look like dancers dressed up as kachina spirits. They are given to children to teach them the parts they play in tribal ceremonies. The kachinas are protective spirits. Parents often hang the dolls above their babies' cradles.

The Pueblo perform many ceremonial dances, such as the Corn Dance and the Turtle Dance, as a prayer for rain or of thanks for a good harvest.

KIVAS

Many ceremonies were carried out in the kivas. The kivas were built underground, so they would be warm in the winter and cool in the summer. The walls of the kivas were decorated with paintings of Kokopelli and other important gods. Every member of a Pueblo village belonged to a kiva society. Pueblo women built the kivas, but only men were allowed inside. Each society was responsible for specific religious ceremonies.

Kivas had flat timber roofs supported by posts. People entered the kiva by climbing down a ladder that was positioned through a hole in the roof.

Music and Dance

Music is an important part of Pueblo life. Children use small drums to learn traditional songs. Drums are made by stretching rawhide across the top of hollowed cottonwood branches. Pueblo children also shake rattles, which are made by filling **gourds** with dried beans.

Traditional Pueblo dances vary from one pueblo village to another. For the most part, dances are part of religious ceremonies performed to ask the gods for rain and good crops.

During the Eagle Dance, Pueblo dancers dress up as eagles. They wear feather armbands and white caps with yellow bills. The dancers make flying movements. This dance is performed because some Pueblo peoples believe the eagle can bring rain by talking to the gods who live above the clouds.

Pueblo dances are a combination of ancient southwestern ceremonies and Catholic celebrations.

CEREMONIAL DANCING

The Hopi perform the Snake Dance. The Hopi believe there are gods who live under the ground. They believe snakes talk to these gods. The snakes ask the gods to provide enough water for the Hopi peoples. As part of the dance to the gods, dancers dress up in red cloths that are painted with a black zigzag pattern. This pattern represents the snakes. Other patterns show footprints of water creatures such as ducks and frogs. During one part of the dance, each dancer carries a live snake in his mouth.

One of the most important Zuni dances is the Shalako dance. During this dance, men wear costumes that represent the gods. The men dance throughout the night in new homes that were built for them in the Zuni village. The following day, they have a race to plant prayer sticks in the ground. Prayer sticks are made from willow that is found by the river. The prayer sticks are carved, painted, and decorated with feathers. The sticks help bring health and **fertility** to the village's crops, people, and animals.

Traditional drums are made from hollowed logs and rawhide.

Language and Storytelling

The Pueblo peoples spoke four languages. The languages were Hopi, Zuni, Keres, and Tano. Over time, they developed into six languages: Hopi, Zuni, Keresan, Tiwa, Towa, and Tewa. Tiwa, Towa, and Tewa are dialects of the Tano language. A dialect is the new language that is formed when people make slight changes to a language. The **pronunciation** or meaning of some of the words may be changed. The Zuni language is not spoken in any other region. It is a distinct language. Today, Pueblo peoples also speak English, and many speak Spanish, too.

Thousands of years ago, the Pueblo peoples painted pictures on rock walls to tell stories. These paintings are called pictographs.

The Pueblo peoples enjoyed telling stories for entertainment as well as to teach lessons about the past. To help tell these stories, they made dolls, which represented the characters. The coyote was a popular figure in their stories.

Each pueblo community has its own myth to explain such mysteries as the creation of Earth. As a result, creation stories differ from one pueblo to another. However, they have some common features. For example, Sun Father, Moon Mother, and the creation of the first people on Earth are common to all Pueblo creation stories.

One of the most important figures in Pueblo myths or legends is Kokopelli. Drawings of Kokopelli appear on caves, pottery, and inside kiva walls. Traditions vary between pueblos, but Kokopelli is usually shown as a humpbacked man with a flute. By performing ceremonies, the Pueblo were asking Kokopelli to bring rain and good crops. Some people believed that Kokopelli would bring fertility to humans and livestock. Kokopelli used his flute to talk to the gods and ask for the things people wanted. He used the hump on his back to bring gifts to the world.

Clay Pueblo storytellers represent tribal elders who tell stories to Pueblo children.

Pueblo Art

The Pueblo are well known for their pottery, baskets, jewelry, and blankets. Each Pueblo community uses unique patterns in their pottery, baskets, and weaving.

Traditionally, the Pueblo peoples used a coil method to make pottery. This artistic tradition continues today. Potters roll clay into long, narrow coils. They place the coils on top of one another to form a pot. Then potters smooth the coils to make a flat surface. They paint designs or carve patterns on the pot. Finally, they fire the pots. Traditionally, the Pueblo fired pots in outdoor pits, using pinion and juniper trees as fire fuel. Today, they fire pots in electric kilns. Some Pueblo potters make pottery that is black in color. Others are known for making pure white pottery, or mixing the styles and using different colors.

The Pueblo used various plants to make baskets. The different colors of these plants produced many patterns. Basket makers still use a traditional method to make baskets. The basket maker begins by joining several pieces of **cattail**, which have been soaked in water.

The Pueblo did not sell pottery to tourists until the 1800s.

Puebloans made rock art called pictographs. Scientists believe pictographs tell stories about the Pueblo's life and religious beliefs.

The cattails are wrapped with willow, and twisted into a coil on the bottom of the basket. An **awl** is used to pierce holes and pull willow around the cattail coil. This pattern continues as the basket maker builds the sides of the basket. Basket makers also create baskets in square designs.

Pueblo men and women have been weaving since about A.D. 800. The Ancestral Puebloans (Anasazi) used plant fibers, such as cotton and yucca, to weave. They wove bags, belts, blankets, clothing, footwear, and hats. Later, they began to weave with wool. The Pueblo peoples invented the upright weaving looms. Sometimes the Pueblo include weaving as part of religious ceremonies.

ROCK ART

In early times, Pueblo artists mixed paints using mineral or plant **pigments** and applied them to walls with a yucca leaf brush. They used the same patterns and designs to decorate pottery and the kiva.

Petroglyphs are pictures American Indians, such as the Pueblo, carved into rock walls. These pictures recorded stories and myths. Sharp stone tools were used to chisel animal and human images into the rock. Petroglyphs can still be seen in the Four Corners region.

One example of this cliff art is found at the entrance to the Needles District of Canyonlands. It is called Newspaper Rock. Images of animal pelts, horses, riders, and people are drawn on the rock. Early Pueblo peoples created the rock carvings on this wall about 1,500 years ago. Scientists do not clearly understand the meaning of these symbols.

Zuni Fetishes

The Zuni peoples believed that during the creation of the world, the Sun God's twin sons used lightning to turn animals into stones. The Zuni believed the animals' spirits were kept alive inside these stones. They thought the stones had special powers that could be used to protect the Zuni from other animals. The Zuni peoples believe that each **fetish** maintained the characteristics of the animal it resembled. People hunted for stones that looked like animals. They had the stones blessed by a **medicine man**. These blessed animal-shaped stones were called fetishes. Zuni peoples also carved fetishes out of hard items, such as stones and shells.

Fetishes were believed to bring luck, power, and protection. Zuni peoples used fetishes for healing and hunting, as well as for spiritual and ceremonial reasons. Fetishes have become an important art form in the Zuni community. About 400 Zuni artists still make fetishes. A favorite saying taught to all children is "take care of the fetish and it will take care of you."

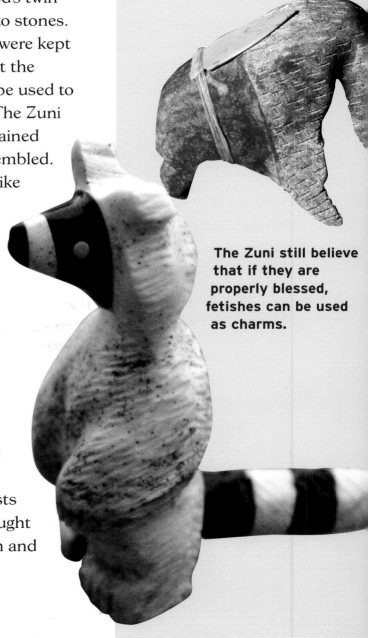

The Zuni still believe that if they are properly blessed, fetishes can be used as charms.

MODERN ARTIST

Cliff Fragua

Cliff Fragua is a Pueblo sculptor from Jemez, New Mexico. He has been sculpting stone since 1974. Fragua's mother and sister are well-known potters. His grandmother made pottery, too. Fragua learned how to make clay pottery, but preferred to work with stone. He studied sculpting in New Mexico, San Francisco, and Italy.

For Fragua, stone expresses the Native values of honesty and purity. Before he begins a sculpture, Fragua carefully examines the stone. He observes its color. He also listens to the sound the stone makes when he taps it. A solid stone makes a ringing sound. Fragua calls this singing. For this reason, Fragua named his studio the Singing Stone Studio.

Fragua works with bronze as well as stone. Many of his sculptures are human figures carved with smooth, flowing lines. His work combines Pueblo traditions with modern culture.

Fragua has won many awards for his work. In 1995, he won the Wheelwright Museum Award of Excellence in Sculpture at the Southwestern Association for Indian Arts (SWAIA) Annual Indian Market. In 1998, he won the Best of Show award at the Native American Artists Invitational.

In 2000, Fragua was invited to create a sculpture to represent New Mexico at the U.S. Capitol in Washington, D.C. This sculpture will stand in the National Statuary Hall.

Cliff Fragua's work can be seen in the Albuquerque International Airport, the Albuquerque Museum, the Indian Pueblo Cultural Center, and Phoenix City Hall.

In addition to being a sculptor, Fragua is active in the arts community. He has been a board member of the Southwestern Association for Indian Arts, and a member of the Indigenous Sculptor Society. He was President of the Indian Arts & Crafts Association, and Vice-Chairman of the Indian Arts and Crafts Foundation. He has taught sculpture for several years. He remains dedicated to promoting Native arts, artists, and culture.

Studying the Pueblo Peoples' Past

Archaeologists study items left by cultures from the past. Pueblo peoples from the past left many items behind. Archaeologists have been able to study these items to learn more about the Pueblo peoples.

Archaeologists have also explored the ancient ruins of Pueblo villages. They have found proof that the Anasazi were the ancestors of today's modern Pueblo people. These Ancestral Puebloans lived in the area between 100 B.C. and A.D. 1300. They lived in caves or built shelters using wood poles and adobe mud. The Anasazi hunted animals for food, gathered wild plants, and grew squash and corn. They wove baskets and made pottery.

The Pueblo peoples used to shape stone into blocks. They would build large villages with four or five layers of houses. Each village had its own method of putting the rocks and mud together. On some very old houses, archaeologists have found the fingerprints of the people who smeared the mud on the walls.

Archaeologists use special tools to carefully dig up ancient Pueblo artifacts.

TIME LINE

Paleo-Indian Period
Pre-10,000 - 6500 B.C.

Hunted animals and gathered wild plants; made large spearpoints; did not live in permanent settlements.

Archaic
6500 - 1500 B.C.

Hunted animals and gathered wild plants; used natural shelters, and made temporary structures; used spear throwers and darts; wove some items, such as sandals; moved with the changing of the seasons.

Basketmaker
1500 B.C. - A.D. 750

Hunted and gathered for most food; limited farming of corn, beans, and squash; began settling and building permanent houses; wove detailed baskets; began making pottery; bow and arrow began to be used.

Pueblo I Period
A.D. 750 - 900

Began building large villages; included storage and living rooms and deep pit structures in houses; used wood and adobe to build; began decorating pottery.

Pueblo II Period
A.D. 900 - 1150

Started using stone for construction; connected above-ground houses making them larger; ceremonial chamber developed into the kiva; made pottery of many shapes and styles.

Pueblo III Period
A.D. 1150 - 1300

Built large pueblos in some areas; spread out to other places including central Utah, southern California, and northern Mexico.

Pueblo IV Period
A.D. 1300 - 1600

Developed large villages of plaza-type pueblos; pottery became less detailed.

Pueblo V Period
1600 - present

Began raising cattle, goats, horses, and sheep; wool replaced cotton for cloth; grew corn, beans, cotton, melon, squash, and chili peppers instead of gathering.

Handicrafts and tourism helped people make a living alongside agriculture. Many modern Pueblo peoples moved into nearby modern homes, though some kept their traditional pueblo homes, as well.

Hand Stamping

Long ago, Pueblo peoples made handprints called pictographs on cave walls. This is one of the methods they used.

STEP 1 Pueblo peoples gathered white clay from a riverbank. They removed all the rocks and sticks from the clay.

STEP 2 They mixed the white clay with water, until it became a smooth paint-like mixture.

STEP 3 They dipped their hand in the liquid clay and placed it flat against the wall.

STEP 4 With their hand pressed against the wall, they blew air around it to harden the clay mixture. This left a handprint on the wall.

Try making handprints like the Pueblo peoples. Place your hand on a piece of construction paper and paint around your hand with a brush. Next, do the same with your other hand. Now you have your own pictograph.

Pueblo people also dipped their hands into the white clay and pressed them on the rock wall, leaving a white handprint. You could try this method with paint and paper, too.

Further Reading

Many of the historical resources available about American Indians were written by authors who did not understand their cultures. An accurate and modern account that includes correct information is *The Jumanos* by Nancy Hickerson, University of Texas Press, 1994. Jumanos are Texan Pueblo peoples.

A factual look at the daily life and artistry of a Puebloan family is told in *Children of Clay: A Family of Pueblo Potters* by Pueblo author Rina Swentzell, Lerner Publications, 1993.

Web Sites

Take a trip through time with the Pueblo peoples at: **www.crowcanyon.org/kids.html**

You can learn about the meaning, history, and current events of Pueblo art at: **www.americanart.si.edu/education/guides/pueblo/pueblo_bios.html**

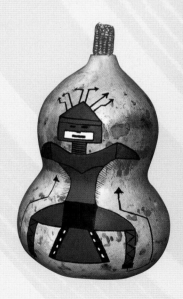

Learn about the archaeological history of the Pueblo people at: **www.dragonflydream.com/PuebloIndians.html**

You can learn about the history of Pueblo peoples at: **www.puebloindian.com**

GLOSSARY

adobe: red mud that is used to make bricks

ancestors: relatives who lived a very long time ago

archaeologists: scientists who study objects from the past to learn about people who lived long ago

awl: a sharp tool used for making holes in soft materials

cattail: a tall rush with long, flat leaves and flowers

council: a group of community leaders who give advice and make decisions for the entire community

dialects: variations on a language that is spoken in a certain place

fertility: the ability to have many children or for a field to grow much food

fetish: a stone carving of an animal, which is carried for luck

gourds: vegetables that have a hard skin and can be hollowed out

gypsum: a mineral used to make plaster products

harmony: getting along with one's surroundings

irrigate: a method of supplying water to crops

kachinas: carved wooden dolls that represent gods and are given to children for good luck

kiva: a round underground room that is used for ceremonies

lance: a long, wooden spear

looms: wooden frames that are used for weaving

mantas: blankets with one strap over the right shoulder

medicine man: someone who has the power to cure illnesses and can communicate with spirits

mesas: flat-topped pieces of land that are high above the rest of the land

obsidian: a kind of glassy black stone

petroglyphs: designs or pictures carved into rock

pigments: colored compounds used in paints and dyes

plaza: a central area in a village, which is used for gathering, working, and playing

possess: to influence or control

pronunciation: a way of speaking a word

Puebloans: Pueblo peoples

turquoise: a bluish-green gemstone

yucca: a low shrub that can be used for cloth fibers, sharp needles, and paint brushes

INDEX